WORLD IN
FOCUS

FOCUS ON THE
United States

SALLY GARRINGTON

WORLD ALMANAC® LIBRARY

Please visit our web site at: www.worldalmanaclibrary.com
For a free color catalog describing World Almanac® Library's list of high-quality books
and multimedia programs, call 1-800-848-2928 (USA) or 1-800-387-3178 (Canada).
World Almanac® Library's fax: (414) 332-3567.

Library of Congress Cataloging-in-Publication Data

Garrington, Sally.
    Focus on the United States / by Sally Garrington.
        p. cm. — (World in focus)
    Includes bibliographical references and index.
    ISBN 0-8368-6725-4 (lib. bdg.)
    ISBN 0-8368-6732-7 (softcover)
    1. United States—Juvenile literature. I. Garrington, Sally. II. Title. III. World in focus
(Milwaukee, Wis.)
    E156.B76   2007
    973—dc22   2006002660

This North American edition first published in 2007 by
World Almanac® Library
A Member of the WRC Media Family of Companies
330 West Olive Street, Suite 100
Milwaukee, WI 53212 USA

This U.S. edition copyright © 2007 by World Almanac® Library. Original edition copyright
© 2005 by Hodder Wayland. First published in 2005 by Hodder Wayland, an imprint of
Hodder Children's Books, a division of Hodder Headline Limited, 338 Euston Road,
London NW1 3BH, U.K.

Commissioning editor: Victoria Brooker
Editor: Nicola Barber
Inside design: Chris Halls, www.mindseyedesign.co.uk
Cover design: Wayland
Series concept and project management by EASI-Educational Resourcing (info@easi-er.co.uk)
Statistical research: Anna Bowden

World Almanac® Library editor: Alan Wachtel
World Almanac® Library cover design: Scott Krall

Population Density Map © 2003 UT-Battelle, LLC. All rights reserved.
Data for population density maps reproduced under licence from UT-Battelle, LLC.
All rights reserved.
Maps and graphs: Martin Darlison, Encompass Graphics

Picture acknowledgements:
The author and publisher would like to thank the following for allowing their pictures to be reproduced in this publication: Corbis 5
(Bruce Burkhardt), 6 (Ricky Flores/The Journal News), 8, 9, 10 and 11 (Bettmann), 12 (Hulton-Deutsch Collection), 13 (Peter
Turnley), 14 (John and Lisa Merrill), 15 (Irwin Thompson/Dallas Morning News), 16 (Gunter Marx), *cover bottom* and 17 (Theo
Allofs/zefa), 18 (Paul Barton), 19 (David H. Wells), 20 (Lester Lefkowitz), *cover top* and 22 (William Manning), 23 (Brooks Kraft),
24 (Fred Prouser/Reuters), 25 (Judy Sloan), 26 (Orjan F. Ellingvag), 27 (Dave G. Houser/Post-Houserstock), 28 (Nathan Benn), 30
(Alison Wright), 31 (Tom Bean), 32 (Frederic Larson), 33 (Jeff Topping/Reuters), 34 (G. Boutin/zefa), 35 (Chris Barth/Star Ledger), 36
(Macduff Everton), 37 (Kevin Coombs/Reuters), 38 (Handout/Reuters), 39 (K. Hackenberg/zefa), *title page*, 40 and 50 (Buddy Mays),
41 (Jack Kurtz/ZUMA), 42 (Karen Kasmauski), 44 (Ed Kashi), 45 (Saed Hindash/Star Ledger), 46 and 59 (Reuters), 47 (Mike Zens),
48 (Allen T. Jules), 49 (Jeff Christensen/Reuters), 51 (Tony Arruza), 52 (Karl Weatherly), 53 (Duomo), 54 (Nik Wheeler), 55 (Will &
Deni McIntyre), 56 (Daniel J. Cox); 57 (Jim Sugar), 58 (Kevin Dodge), Chris Fairclough 4, 21, 29 and 43.

The directional arrow portrayed on the map on page 7 provides only an approximation of north.
The data used to produce the graphics and data panels in this title were the latest available at the time of production.

Printed in China

1 2 3 4 5 6 7 8 9 10 09 08 07 06

CONTENTS

Cover: A cable car in San Francisco, California.

Title page: A family camping in Sawtooth National Forest, in Idaho.

CHAPTER 1

The United States – An Overview

The United States of America is the world's third largest country in terms of area (after Russia and Canada) and the world's most powerful country in terms of its economy and involvement in world affairs. The country was born in 1776, when American colonists declared themselves independent from Britain. Since that time, the lure of a new life in the United States has attracted millions of immigrants from countries all over the world, and today the United States has one of the most diverse populations of any country. Plentiful land, vast natural resources, and the ideals and hard work of its citizens have helped to build the United States into the world's only superpower of the early twenty-first century.

The influence of the United States spreads far beyond its borders. The country has used its military and economic power to intervene in conflicts around the world, often defending or assisting peoples in need. Its influence extends into the lives of billions of people who benefit from its scientific advances and cultural richness. American developments in medicine and technology help shape life in the United States and beyond. Common features of American life—from Coca Cola to rock 'n' roll, and from Hollywood movies to hip-hop—have become part of the culture of the world.

A HUGE COUNTRY

Almost two-and-a-half times the area of the 25-member European Union, and 40 times the size of Britain, the United States is made up of 50 states. Two of these—Hawaii, in the South Pacific, and Alaska, located to the northwest of Canada—are geographically separated from the other 48. Including Alaska, the United States has a northern border with Canada of 5,526 miles (8,893 kilometers), while to its south it shares a border with Mexico of 1,952 miles (3,141 km). To the west of the country is the Pacific Ocean, and to its east lies the Atlantic

◀ This crowd in New York City shows some of the ethnic diversity of the American people.

▲ Many American students say the Pledge of Allegiance at the beginning of each school day.

Ocean, across which early settlers migrated from Europe. The Gulf of Mexico lies to the south of the country, along the states of Texas, Louisiana, Mississippi, Alabama, and Florida.

NATURAL RESOURCES

The United States straddles latitudes stretching from just above the Tropic of Cancer in the south to beyond the Arctic Circle in the north. This area includes many types of landscapes and climates, and a variety of natural resources including timber, natural gas, uranium, copper, and oil. The exploitation of these resources over the last four hundred years has helped the United States to grow wealthy. In certain areas of the country, however, use of resources has led to considerable damage to the environment.

In addition to exploiting its own resources, the United States also imports resources from abroad,

especially in cases in which its own supplies don't meet its needs. The country is particularly dependent on imported oil. In 2004, the United States consumed 20.517 million barrels of oil per day, 65 percent of which were imported. Trade for resources is one part of the country's complex relationships with the rest of the world.

A MILITARY SUPERPOWER

The immense wealth of the United States has given it great military power, and it has been involved in most of the major world conflicts over the last 90 years. In the late twentieth and early twenty-first centuries, the United States has been involved—both militarily and diplomatically—in conflicts in the Middle East. The country is working to bring democratic government and stability to Iraq, after it led the invasion that toppled Saddam Hussein in 2003. It is also keeping a watchful eye on the threats posed by nuclear proliferation, and on the conflict between Israel and the Palestinians, with the hope that it can aid a peaceful solution.

The role the United States has played on the world stage, however, has angered some groups of extremists, making the country a target for terrorists. On September 11, 2001, al-Qaeda terrorists killed about 3,000 people, destroyed the World Trade Center, and damaged the Pentagon in an attack that used four hijacked planes as giant bombs. In response, the United States overthrew the Taliban government of Afghanistan, which harbored al-Qaeda, and continues to hunt the group's leaders.

A FREE COUNTRY

Since it was founded, the United States has always drawn to its shores large numbers of immigrants, attracted by the religious and

political freedoms and the economic opportunities the country offers. This constant influx of people helps to give the country an exciting energy. The United States is a land of contrasts and unity at the same time. Its fifty states are united by one Constitution. Its people—who differ dramatically in ethnicity, religion, political views, and economic status— are all guaranteed the same basic rights of life, liberty, and the pursuit of happiness.

 Did You Know?

The Statue of Liberty—which stands in New York Harbor and is one of the most well-known symbols of the United States—was a gift from the people of France in 1886. It represents political and individual freedoms.

Physical Geography

- Land area: 3,536,502 square miles/ 9,161,923 square kilometers
- Water area: 181,225 sq miles/ 469,495 sq km
- Total area: 3,717,727 sq miles/ 9,631,418 sq km
- World rank (by area): 3
- Land boundaries: 7,478 miles/12,034 km
- Border countries: Canada, Mexico
- Coastline: 12,381 miles/19,924 km
- Highest point: Mount McKinley (20,322 feet/ 6,194 meters)
- Lowest point: Death Valley (-282 ft/-86 m)

Source: CIA World Factbook

◀ New York City firefighters raise the American flag at the site of the World Trade Center after the terrorist attacks of September 11, 2001.

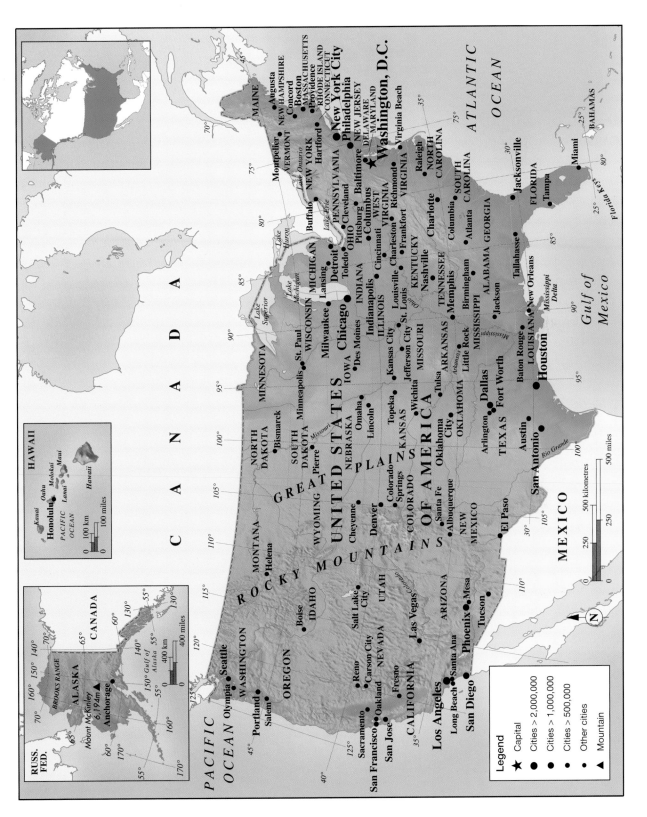

Legend

★ Capital
● Cities > 2,000,000
● Cities > 1,000,000
• Cities > 500,000
· Other cities
▲ Mountain

CHAPTER 2

History

EARLY BEGINNINGS

The first humans to inhabit the land that was to become the United States were the ancestors of today's Native Americans. Theories suggest that they migrated across a land bridge between Asia and America more than 10,000 years ago, when sea levels were much lower. Once in the Americas, they gradually spread south, forming many different groups. European colonization of this land began with the voyage of the Italian-born Spanish navigator Christopher Columbus, who landed in the Caribbean in 1492. By the 17th century, people from Spain, France, England, and the Netherlands had colonized large areas of this "New World."

THE AMERICAN REVOLUTION

By 1763, Britain controlled Canada and all of North America east of the Mississippi River. However, many of the people living in Britain's American colonies had begun to question their treatment by the British government. The colonists were expected to feed and house British troops in the colonies, which was a heavy drain on their incomes. Britain levied heavy taxes on the colonists, including taxes on many goods that needed to be imported such as sugar, coffee, tea and wine. Many colonists resented paying these taxes, particularly because they had no representation in the British parliament. The American Revolution began in 1775 when

 Did You Know?

Thanksgiving, held every year in the United States on the fourth Thursday in November, has its origins in the festival to give thanks for the safe gathering of the harvest held by early English settlers in North America.

▶ Modern-day Americans take part in a re-enactment of the first Thanksgiving in Plymouth, Massachusetts, when Native Americans and settlers joined together to give thanks for a successful harvest.

▶ In this detail from a painting by John Trumbull (1756–1843), representatives of the thirteen colonies sign the Declaration of Independence on July 4, 1776.

many colonists decided to break free from British rule. During this war, the Declaration of Independence was signed on July 4, 1776, by representatives of the 13 British colonies. The British sent troops to prevent the colonies from enacting this declaration, but the British eventually lost the war, surrendering in Yorktown, Virginia, in 1781.

THE NEW NATION

Under the Articles of Confederation, drawn up in 1781, the colonies tried to work together as the United States of America, but the Articles failed to establish an effective federal government. In 1787, the Articles were abandoned and a new Constitution was written. The aim of the Constitution—and the Bill of Rights that was added in 1791—was to safeguard individual freedoms and to organize the country without giving too much power to a centralized government. The first president to head the government was George Washington,

who, in 1789, was unanimously elected by representatives from all the states.

EXPANDING WESTWARD

During the first half of the 19th century, the United States expanded steadily westward across the North American continent. In 1803, the U.S. government bought Louisiana from France, extending its territory as far west as the Rocky Mountains. But as American settlers moved west they often came into conflict with Native American groups who had lived on these lands for thousands of years. The U.S. government sent troops to deal with the Native Americans, and many had their lands taken away by force. In 1838, the 15,000 members of the Cherokee tribe were ordered to leave their lands in Georgia and make the 1,000-mile (1,600-km) journey to Oklahoma. About 4,000 Cherokee died on this terrible march, which came to be known as the "Trail of Tears."

FREE AND SLAVE STATES

Black slaves imported from Africa had been put to work in America since the middle of the 17th century. Slavery, however, was at odds with the Declaration of Independence, which stated that "all men are created equal." Many Americans called for the end of slavery. By the early 19th century, all northern states ("free" states) had outlawed slavery. But, in the southern states ("slave" states), which relied on slave labor on plantations, the practice of owning slaves was fiercely protected. A balance between free states and slave states had been struck, but in 1820, the state of Missouri applied to be admitted to the United States as a slave state. In order to avoid throwing off the balance between free states and slave states in the government, the Missouri Compromise was created to allow the admission of both Missouri as a slave state and the newly created state of Maine, in the north, as a free state. For a short time, this arrangement maintained the balance of power between the two factions.

THE CIVIL WAR

The compromise between free and slave states came under pressure after the end of the Mexican-American War of 1848. Under the treaty that ended the war, the United States gained large areas of new territory, but the question arose about whether the new states created out of this territory should be free states or slave states. After years of attempted compromise and disagreements, matters came to a head in 1861 when 11 southern states seceded from the United States to form the Confederate States of America after the election of President Abraham Lincoln (1809–1865), who was an opponent of slavery. Despite Lincoln's attempts to keep the country together, this split was the beginning of the Civil War, a bloody battle between the northern (Union) and southern (Confederate) armies. The Union won the war in 1865, and the 13th Amendment to the Constitution outlawed slavery throughout the United States. It was to be many more years, however, before descendants of the freed slaves were given full civil rights.

► This photograph, taken in June 1862, shows four Union soldiers grouped around their cannon near Fair Oaks, Virginia.

BEGINNING OF THE MODERN NATION

After the end of Civil War, the Industrial Revolution brought rapid development of the oil, textile, steel, and mining industries in the United States. The country's world influence through manufactured goods had begun. Its role as a major world power also grew with its support of the Allies (Britain, France, Russia, and Italy) in World War I (1914–1918).

In 1929, the U.S. economy suffered a major setback with the financial collapse of the New York Stock Market on Wall Street. The value of the U.S. dollar fell, and many people's savings became worthless overnight. High unemployment and rapidly rising prices led to a period in the 1930s known as the Great Depression. The Depression lasted until the United States entered World War II (1939–1945) in support of the Allies (Britain, France, and Russia) after its naval base at Pearl Harbor was bombed by Japan in 1941. To supply the vast war effort, American factories and farms went into full production, producing great amounts of weapons, vehicles, and food. The effect of this was a doubling of the country's manufacturing output and a rapid reduction in unemployment. The United States fought with the Allies in Europe against the armies of Nazi Germany and also in the Pacific against Japan. Nearly 300,000 U.S. soldiers lost their lives during these conflicts. In 1945, the United States dropped atomic bombs on the Japanese cities of Hiroshima and Nagasaki, which ended the war in the Pacific but had devastating and long-lasting effects on Japan.

▼ Protesters in front of the Capitol building, in Washington, D. C., in 1932, during the Great Depression. Over 12,000 people traveled from Pittsburgh, Pennsylvania, for the protest.

THE COLD WAR

After World War II, the United States became a founding member of the United Nations (UN) and took a lead role in world politics. The United States felt that communism, especially as practiced by the Soviet Union, was a serious threat to world peace. Great political hostility existed between the two countries, but because no direct military conflict between them occurred, this period became known as the "Cold War." The United States, however, was involved in two wars intended to prevent the spread of communism. The first was the Korean War (1950–1953), which ended in a stalemate that left Korea divided into communist North Korea and democratic South Korea. Beginning in about 1965, the United States was heavily involved in the war in Vietnam. The United States gave support, including troops, to South Vietnam in its fight against communist forces from North Vietnam. Increasing costs in terms of money and the lives of soldiers—along with the fact that this was the first time that television cameras brought the reality of war into people's homes—led many Americans to protest the war. The Vietnam War ended in 1973 after a settlement and the withdrawal of U.S. troops.

THE IMPORTANCE OF OIL

After World War II, the United States became increasingly dependent on oil to fuel its industries, transportation, and homes. In 1973,

Focus on: The Civil Rights Movement

The movement to bring full civil rights and equality to African-Americans started in the 19th century. But even after World War II, education and public transportation in some southern states remained segregated by race. A campaign of protests and boycotts throughout the 1950s and 1960s resulted in desegregation and important legislation to end racial discrimination. In the 1960s, Martin Luther King Jr., one of the most prominent civil rights leaders, spoke of his dream of a country where all would live together in peace. He was assassinated in 1968. Today, the civil rights movement continues to work against racial discrimination in U.S. society.

▲ Martin Luther King Jr. waves from the Lincoln Memorial, in Washington, D. C., to people taking part in a civil rights march held on August 28,1963.

in retaliation for the West's support of Israel, the Arab countries cut off oil supplies to the United States, Japan, and Western Europe. This crisis highlighted the importance to the United States of the oil supply from the countries of the Middle East. When Iraq invaded Kuwait in 1990, the United States, along with many other countries, fought the Gulf War to liberate Kuwait and keep its considerable oil reserves accessible.

THE WAR ON TERROR

With the breakup of the Soviet Union in 1991, the United States became the world's only superpower. As it came into this position of global dominance, some of its enemies, particularly radical Islamic groups such as al-Qaeda, became increasingly militant in opposing U.S. influence. The terrorist attacks of September 11, 2001, prompted U.S. president George W. Bush to declare a "war on terror."

▲ A U.S. soldier stands on a destroyed Iraqi tank in 1991, during the Gulf War. In the background are burning Kuwaiti oil wells that were set on fire by Iraq's retreating army.

Late in 2001, the United States and a large international coalition took action against terrorist forces and their sponsors in Afghanistan. Several countries, however, expressed strong disapproval of the U.S.-led invasion of Iraq that took place in 2003 and toppled the regime of Saddam Hussein. Today, the United States, along with Britain and other countries, is working to establish democratic government in Iraq, but its actions in Iraq have been questioned by many people around the world, including many Americans who resent the loss of young American lives in the conflict and believe the U.S. government's case for going to war was weak.

CHAPTER 3

Landscape and Climate

The United States covers 3,536,502 sq miles (9,161,923 sq km) and incorporates many different landscapes. The country has two main mountain ranges. The Appalachians are located in the east of the country and include the Blue Ridge Mountains. In the west are the great Rocky Mountains, which include several peaks over 13,120 feet (4,000 m). Between these two mountain ranges lie the Great Plains, where altitude rarely reaches 1,312 ft (400 m). Many rivers drain this area, including the Mississippi and its tributaries. Alaska, lying to the northwest of Canada, contains the tallest peak in the United States, Mount McKinley. Hawaii, separated from the mainland of the United States by 2,386 miles (3,840 km) of ocean, consists of 132 volcanic islands, seven of which are inhabited. It still has active volcanoes, including Mauna Loa. Mauna Loa is 30,080 feet (9,170 m) high from the seabed, making it the highest mountain in the world when measured in this way.

NATURAL HAZARDS

The United States experiences a wide range of natural hazards including tornadoes, wildfires, hurricanes, avalanches, flooding, earthquakes, and volcanic eruptions. Most of its large tornadoes occur in Texas, Oklahoma, Kansas, and Nebraska along an area called "Tornado

▼ Fresh snowfall on Mount McKinley, the highest mountain in the United States. Mount McKinley is located in Denali National Park in Alaska.

Alley." They are very destructive and each year cause about 60 deaths. Hurricanes make landfall in Florida and other southern and southeastern states. The Atlantic hurricane season runs from June to November, while the hurricane season for the Pacific region lasts from May to November. The National Weather Service issues regular reports and warnings about hurricanes and tornadoes.

Most earthquakes and volcanoes occur near the margins of the tectonic plates that form Earth's surface. Earthquakes are common in California because the San Andreas fault, which is the line at which two of these plates meet, runs through the state. In 1994, an earthquake measuring 6.6 on the Richter scale struck Los Angeles, killing 60 people and injuring more than 7,000.

The most spectacular recent volcanic eruption in the United States took place in the Cascade Mountains in the northwest of the country. The perfect cone shape of Mount St. Helens was blown to pieces when the volcano erupted on May 18, 1980, removing 0.65 cubic miles (2.7 cubic km) of its top to leave a vast crater. Forests were flattened by the blast for about 230 square miles (600 sq km) and the ash cloud from the blast closed Seattle's airport and cut out sunlight over the city of Seattle for several days. Fifty-seven people died as a result of the eruption.

 Did You Know?

Located in the northern United States, the Great Lakes contain one-fifth of the world's fresh water.

Focus on: Hurricane Katrina

Hurricane Katrina touched land in Louisiana on August 29, 2005, with wind speeds of up to 200 miles per hour (320 kilometers per hour). It devastated an area of the southern United States the size of Great Britain. Much of the city of New Orleans is below sea level, and when the levees that surround the city broke, two-thirds of the city was flooded. Many people evacuated the city, but those who were unable to leave were stranded for several days without food or clean water. It is estimated that there have been 1,330 deaths caused by Katrina, as well as U.S.$200 billion worth of damage to property and businesses.

▲ A volunteer rescues residents from a local school in Baton Rouge, Louisiana, where they had gone to escape their flooded homes after Hurricane Katrina hit in September 2005.

 Badwater, the lowest point in the United States, is in Death Valley National Park and attracts thousands of tourists every year to view its stark landscapes.

CONTRASTING CLIMATES

Climates in the United States range from the tropical to the arctic. Hawaii, in the South Pacific, has a tropical climate that is hot all year round with the average temperature never falling below 73° F (23° C) and a wet season from October to March. This contrasts with Alaska where almost one-third of the state is inside the Arctic Circle. During December, Alaska has only one hour of daylight and temperatures average -9° F (-23° C). In fact, the average temperature

? Did You Know?

The highest temperature ever recorded in the United States was 134° F (57° C), in Death Valley, in California, in 1913. The lowest temperature ever recorded was -80° F (-62° C) at Prospect Creek, in Alaska, in 1971.

only rises above the freezing point for seven months of the year, and it is too cold in most parts for trees to grow.

Within the 48 states of the continental United States, climates range from hot desert, through arid grasslands, to moist coastal and forest areas. Climates along the coasts are milder than inland because the sea moderates temperatures, preventing them from becoming either very hot or very cold. Florida has a warm, subtropical climate that allows the cultivation of oranges, lemons, and other fruits. California, in the west, has a Mediterranean-type climate with hot, dry summers and mild, damp winters. This climate is ideal for growing grapes and supports California's wine industry. Inland and away from the influence of the sea, states such as Nebraska and Kansas experience very cold winters and very hot summers. This prairie region is one of the world's most important wheat-growing areas.

The Rocky Mountains in the west block the path of rain-bearing westerly winds, forcing the winds to rise and drop their rain. In Oregon and Washington, the heavy rainfall helps large forests to grow. The eastern side of the Rockies is much drier. The Mojave and Sonoran deserts lie in the southwest, where temperatures are higher. Vegetation in this region includes cacti and other plant species, such as blackbrush, that have adapted to the hot, arid conditions.

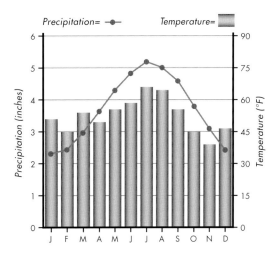

▼ Tourists standing at the South Rim of the Grand Canyon, located in Arizona, look across the canyon.

▲ Average monthly climate conditions in Washington, D. C.

Focus on: The Grand Canyon

In the Grand Canyon, the Colorado River has cut a gorge 1 mile (1.5 km) deep through many different layers of rock. Traveling down from the top of the canyon to the river you pass through four different vegetation and climate zones, from forests of Douglas Fir down to desert at the bottom. It can be snowing at the rim and hot enough for T-shirts at the bottom, with a temperature difference of 30° F (15° C). The range of environments in the Grand Canyon is similar to those found while driving 1,243 miles (2,000 km) from Canada to New Mexico.

CHAPTER 4

Population and Settlements

The United States is the world's third most populous nation, with about 296 million people. Its population is unevenly distributed. The most densely populated region is the northeast, with an average of 1,134 people per square mile (438 people per square km) in the state of New Jersey, compared to an average of just over 6 people per sq mile (2 people per sq km) in Montana. The states of California and Florida have also attracted large concentrations of people, partly because of their pleasant climates and coastal positions. Only 20 percent of the U.S. population lives in rural areas. Of people living in rural areas, 10 percent live on farms and the rest live in small cities and towns.

AN AGING POPULATION

The population of the United States is aging. In 2003, 12 percent of Americans were over 65 years of age, and by 2030 this figure is expected to rise to 20 percent. Life expectancy for men has increased from 66 in 1960 to 75 in 2003. In the same period, life expectancy for women has risen from 73 to 80. The birth rate in the United States is high for a developed country, especially in young immigrant families. In spite of this, the government estimates that, without more immigration, there will be a shortage of workers by 2026, due to a high proportion of the present working population retiring.

Population Data

- Population: 296 million
- Population 0–14 yrs: 21%
- Population 15–64 yrs: 67%
- Population 65+ yrs: 12%
- Population growth rate: 1%
- Population density: 79.9 per sq mile/ 30.8 per sq km
- Urban population: 80%
- Major cities: New York 8,104,079
  Los Angeles 3,845,541
  Chicago 2,862,244

Sources: United Nations, World Bank, World Almanac

◀ Increasing life expectancy in the United States means more active years for many retired people.

IMMIGRATION

Many African Americans, who today make up 12.7 percent of the U.S. population, are descendants of slaves taken from their homelands in the 17th and 18th centuries. However, until the early years of the 20th century, most people coming to the United States came from Europe, initially from countries in northern Europe such as Britain, Ireland, Germany, and Sweden, and later from countries in southern and eastern Europe, particularly Italy. Two million Jews immigrated to the United States between 1880 and 1920 as they fled persecution in Russia and Germany. During the 20th century, increasing numbers of immigrants arrived from Asia and South America. Americans who originate from Latin America and the Caribbean are known as Hispanics or Latinos. Today, the Hispanic community is the fastest-growing minority in the United States. The U.S. Census Bureau estimates that the high birth rate in the Hispanic community, as well as continued immigration, will almost double the Hispanic share of the U.S. population by 2050, increasing it from 12.6 percent to 24.4 percent.

Between 1990 and 2000, the number of well-educated Indians who immigrated to the United States increased by 106 percent. Many were attracted by jobs in high-tech industries in which American companies are having problems recruiting workers. These new migrants have brought fresh ideas and enthusiasm, and are an important resource for the country. The Asian population of the United States also includes people originating from Pakistan, the countries of southeast Asia, Korea, China, and Japan. Asians make up the second fastest-growing segment of the U.S. population and are overwhelmingly concentrated in New York, California, and Hawaii.

Focus on: Illegal Immigration

The U.S.-Mexico border is often referred to as "leaky," as it is impossible to police all 1,952 miles (3,141 km). Illegal Mexican migrants take great risks by trying to cross the desert landscape to enter the United States. But Mexico is a less developed and poorer country than the United States, so many Mexicans are prepared to take the gamble of crossing the border in search of job opportunities and better pay.

▲ An English class for immigrants in Arlington, Virginia. Most immigrants to the United States see learning English as vitally important, but many also continue to speak their native languages.

 Did You Know?

Los Angeles is home to 20 percent of the Hispanic population of the United States.

CITIES AND SUBURBS

Eighty percent of people in the United States live in towns and cities. In 2005, the United States had nine cities with populations of over one million. The fastest growing U.S. cities are in the southwest and include Phoenix, Los Angeles, and San Antonio.

Many American city centers have high levels of air and noise pollution, traffic congestion, and crime. Widespread car ownership allows large numbers of people to choose to live outside city centers and commute long distances to work, resulting in urban sprawl as suburbs are built on the edges of cities. The suburbs are particularly popular with middle-class Americans seeking to have more space and avoid some of the problems of city life. Land is cheaper away from city centers, so many people can afford individual houses with backyards, rather than small, and often very expensive, urban houses and apartments. Many workplaces have also moved outside of city centers, causing further decentralization.

POVERTY

Although it is the world's wealthiest country, poverty can be found in most parts of the United States with some of the poorest communities being in largely rural states such as West Virginia and Mississippi. The greatest concentrations of poverty, however, are found in cities such as Chicago, Detroit, Los Angeles, and New York City. In poor areas of cities such as these, it is common for residents to have difficulties in getting jobs and a good education. These areas often also struggle with a variety of social problems, including high crime rates, gangs, and widespread drug abuse.

Occasionally tensions between urban groups or between residents and police boil over. Riots occurred in Los Angeles in 1992 after a mostly white jury acquitted four police officers of beating Rodney King, a black motorist.

▼ A massive suburban development stretches into the desert on the edge of Las Vegas, Nevada.

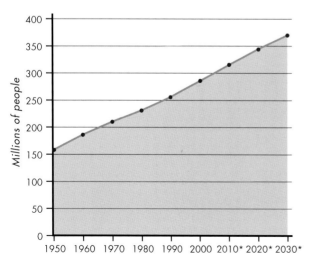

* Projected population

▲ Population growth 1950–2030

LANGUAGES

Even though English is the main language of the United States, many people speak other languages. Spanish is so common that some people consider it the country's second language. Some cities have "Chinatown" areas in which Asian languages are spoken by most people. On the subways of New York City, people can be heard speaking languages ranging from Russian to Arabic to Hebrew.

 Did You Know?

The most populous state in the United States is California. With 36 million people, it has 12 percent of the population living in 4 percent of the total land area. The most populous city is New York City, with just over 18 million people in its metropolitan area.

▼ African Americans in Harlem, a section of New York City known for its black community.

Focus on: Harlem

Harlem is a part of New York City that is a center of African American culture. In the 1920s, it was the scene of the Harlem Renaissance, during which African American art, music, and literature flourished. The Great Depression brought the end of the Harlem Renaissance, and by the 1970s and 1980s, Harlem was known for high crime rates and poorly maintained housing. Since the 1990s, many projects have aimed to rebuild the area and offer new opportunities to its residents, and Harlem has improved greatly. Over the years, it has also become more diverse. The area known as Spanish Harlem was settled by Puerto Ricans in the 1940s and remains a major Hispanic center.

CHAPTER 5

Government and Politics

The United States is a federal republic with a long history of democracy. The people of the United States vote for the leaders they think will best represent them in the government. The basis of government in the United States is the Constitution, which was drawn up in 1787. The writers of the Constitution created three branches of government that would check and balance each other: the executive, the judiciary, and the legislature. Just four years later, in 1791, ten amendments were added to the Constitution that are known as the Bill of Rights. The aim of these amendments is to set out more clearly the rights of the individual citizen, including the three important rights of freedom of speech, freedom of the press, and freedom to follow any chosen religion. They also laid down the right to a jury trial if accused of a crime and the right to bear arms.

GOVERNMENT OF THE UNITED STATES

The executive branch of government is headed by the president of the United States and is in charge of enforcing the laws passed by the legislative branch. It includes departments that deal with areas such as foreign policy, money, education, and agriculture.

▼ Capitol Hill, in Washington, D. C., is the home of the U.S. government. The Capitol building was begun in 1793 and was designed to house the United States Congress.

▲ President George W. Bush stands in the famous Oval Office in the White House, in Washington, D. C., just after his election victory in 2004.

The United States Congress is the country's legislative branch. Members of Congress draw up bills, debate them, and decide which ones will become laws. Congress is made up of the House of Representatives and the Senate. In 2005, the House had 435 members. A state's number of representatives is based on the size of its population. New Hampshire, which has a small population, had two representatives, while Illinois, with a larger population, had nineteen. The Senate has 100 members, with two senators from each state. The reason for this system is to balance power between heavily populated states and those with fewer people. If the president does not agree with a certain bill, it is returned to Congress for further discussion.

The judicial branch of the government acts as a check on the executive and legislative arms in order to ensure they do not violate the Constitution. The judicial branch includes the highest court in the country, the Supreme Court, which has the power to question whether a law or an action by the government goes against the Constitution. It also has power over the lower federal courts.

POLITICAL PARTIES

The United States has two main political parties: the Republicans and the Democrats. The Republicans are viewed as conservative and traditional, while the Democrats are thought of as more liberal and progressive. Inside each party is a wide range of views. Party members do not always follow the party line and may vote with the opposition. It is possible to have a president from one party and a majority in Congress from another, although, this can make passing new laws difficult.

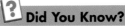

Did You Know?

The symbol of the Republican Party is the elephant, and the symbol of the Democratic Party is the donkey.

FEDERAL AND STATE GOVERNMENTS

The national, overall government of the United States is known as the federal government. Individual states have authority to set their own laws and constitutions to take account of local conditions as long as they don't conflict with federal law. States can make their own laws in areas such as education, criminal justice, and hospital organization. Differences between the laws of various states can cause confusion. For example, in Montana, a 15-year-old can have a full driver's license, but in some states a driver cannot be fully licensed until the age of 18.

ELECTIONS AND THE CITIZEN

Presidential elections in the United States take place every four years, and a president can hold office for a maximum of two terms, or eight years. A presidential campaign normally begins at least a year ahead of the election, and candidates have to raise money to pay for their campaigns. Presidential candidates work hard to create a positive impression on the electorate through the media, including radio, magazines,

▼Voters at a polling station in Burbank, California, mark their ballots in a state election in November 2005.

newspapers, and, above all, television. Senators are elected every six years, and representatives are elected every two years. The reason for this is so one part of Congress can quickly respond to public opinion, while the other can be shielded from sudden changes.

All citizens over the age of 18 are entitled to vote (except for convicted criminals and people judged to be mentally incompetent). Although voting is viewed as a civic duty in the United States, voter turnout is often low.

People from foreign countries who are living in the United States can apply to become U.S. citizens by a process called naturalization. The requirements for naturalization include being of good character, loyal to the United States, and willing to take the Pledge of Allegiance. People applying for naturalization must also be able to read, write, and understand basic English. U.S. citizens have responsibilities as well as rights. Citizens must pay their taxes, and young men are required to register to be called up for military service if necessary.

Focus on: Capital Punishment

As of 2006, there were 38 U.S. states in which criminals can receive the death penalty and 12 in which they cannot. Between 1976 and October 2005, 985 people were executed in the United States. During that time, however, 119 people were found innocent (or freed from blame) while waiting on death row. In 2005, California had over 600 criminals on death row—more than any other state. Between 1982 and 2005, California executed only 12 people. In contrast, over 350 people were executed in Texas—three times more than in any other state.

◀ A woman takes the Oath of Naturalization as part of a ceremony held in the Broward County Convention Center, in Florida, in September 2000. Taking this oath is the last stage in becoming a naturalized citizen of the United States.

CHAPTER 6

Energy and Resources

The United States has a wealth of natural resources, including minerals, forests, fish, land, and water. It also benefits from some of the world's largest reserves of oil, coal, and gas. Even with these resources, the United States does not have enough energy resources to meet the demands of its population and industries.

ENERGY RESOURCES

The American lifestyle is energy-hungry. Many people have homes that are centrally heated in winter, air-conditioned in summer, and equipped with numerous labor-saving machines and gadgets, all of which depend on energy. In addition, many Americans depend on cars. The brightly lit skylines of modern American cities use tremendous amounts of electricity.

 Did You Know?

In 2005, there were 50 percent more cars on the road in the United States than in the 1970s. Today's cars, however, are more fuel-efficient.

In 2004, the economy of the United States consumed over 20 million barrels of oil a day but produced only seven million barrels. The country's shortfall in production is made up by oil imports from Canada, the Middle East, West Africa, Central America, and South America. The Middle East supplies about 20 percent of the oil used in the United States.

One-third of coal mined in the United States comes from the state of Wyoming. The United States is self-sufficient in coal, and coal is the main fuel for the country's electricity production, providing 51 percent of national output. The United States produces natural gas as a fuel, but it also imports gas from Canada in order to keep up with consumption. There are about 306,000 miles (489,600 km) of gas pipeline across the country, distributing the fuel. Using 104 reactors, nuclear power plants produce 20 percent of the country's electricity. Although nuclear power neither produces greenhouse gases nor contributes to global climate change, people worry about nuclear wastes.

◀ This pump extracts oil from rocks beneath a golf course in Houston, Texas.

Alternatives to fossil fuels used in the United States include hydroelectric (HEP), solar, tidal, wind, and geothermal power sources. In states such as California and Florida, which have a great deal of sunshine, banks of photovoltaic panels harness the sun's energy to generate electricity. Wind power accounts for only two percent of electricity produced by renewable means, but it is the fastest growing sector. The wind farm at the San Gorgonio Mountain Pass, California, has over 4,000 turbines and generates enough electricity for the town of Palm Springs and its surrounding area. The newest wind turbines are 305 feet (93 meters) tall—almost the height of the Statue of Liberty—and can each provide electricity for 500 homes.

▲ The vast wind farm in California's San Gorgonio Mountain Pass provides a clean, nonpolluting energy source.

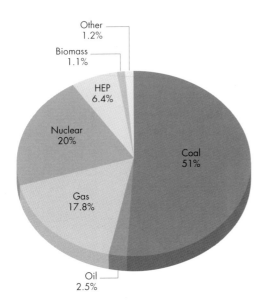

▲ Electricity production by type

Focus on: Hydrogen-fueled cars

The United States produces nine million tons of hydrogen a year. This hydrogen is used in industry and by NASA (National Aeronautics and Space Administration) as a rocket fuel. In the future, however, it may be used to fuel cars. Hydrogen-fueled cars are being developed in U.S. universities in partnership with car companies. The great advantage of hydrogen-fueled cars is that they will have almost zero emissions. One problem with using hydrogen to run cars is the huge expense of converting gas stations to be able to provide hydrogen.

METALS AND MINERALS

The United States mines large amounts of a variety of metals and minerals, and it is the second biggest producer of copper ore, after Chile. Nearly all (99 percent) U.S. copper production is in Arizona, Utah, and New Mexico. The United States produces large amounts of aluminum, one-third of which comes from recycling used aluminum. The same is true of lead: 75 percent of U.S. lead production is from recycled car batteries, while only 25 percent is newly mined. The United States produces one-fifth of the world's sulphur, which is mined mainly along the coasts of Texas and Louisiana, and is used in the making of chemicals.

FORESTS AND FISHING

About 33 percent of the United States is covered with forest, with large areas of forest growing on the western side of the nation. Most of the western forest is owned by the federal government, and nearly one-quarter of it is protected. In contrast, 83 percent of the forests of the eastern United States are privately owned. Most of the country's timber harvesting takes place in the eastern forests.

▼ At Port Sulphur, on the Louisiana coast, sulphur is pumped from underground mines using high-pressure hot water and is then left to cool and solidify.

During 2003, nearly 4.4 million tons (4 million metric tons) of fish were landed in the United States. The most productive fishing areas in the country are in Alaska, where 56 percent of the country's catch is landed, and Louisiana, which produces 13 percent of the total catch.

WATER RESOURCES

The United States has several large rivers. The Mississippi is the country's longest river, at 2,340 miles (3,740 km), and it drains a total of 1,606 square miles (4,160 square km). The southwest of the country is arid, yet it has cities with large populations, such as Las Vegas, Phoenix, and Los Angeles, that require vast amounts of water. Los Angeles takes up 6 percent of the land area of California and is home to 45 percent of the state's population, but it has only 0.6 percent of the state's river flow. It is, therefore, dependent on piping in water from distant locations, which alters river ecosystems and reduces water resources for other settlements.

Focus on: The Colorado River

The Colorado River's name means "red river," and it rises in the Rockies and passes through much of the arid southwest. It is an important resource for the communities along its route as a drinking water supply, irrigation source, and producer of HEP. In fact, nearly all of its water is used up in the United States before it reaches the Gulf of California in Mexico. This has led to tensions between Mexico and the United States, as Mexico feels it should be able to use some of the river's water as a resource.

Energy Data

- Energy consumption as % of world total: 23.4%
- Energy consumption by sector (% of total):
  Industry: 24.3%
  Transportation: 40.8%
  Agriculture: 0.9%
  Services: 12.4%
  Residential: 17.2%
  Other: 4.4%
- CO_2 emissions as % of world total: 24.1%
- CO_2 emissions per capita in tons per year: 22

Source: World Resources Institute

▶ Fish being weighed at the old Fulton Street Fish Market in New York City.

CHAPTER 7

Economy and Income

The United States is an advanced industrialized nation with an enormous service sector (accounting for about 76 percent of employment) and a highly productive manufacturing sector. As manufacturing has become more automated, it has required fewer workers, and the number now working in manufacturing has fallen to just 22 percent of the workforce. Agriculture in the United States accounts for only 2 percent of employment and is a highly mechanized and efficient industry. All of this activity makes the United States the wealthiest nation in the world. In spite of the country's wealth, more than 12 percent of its population lives in poverty, and the divide between the wealthy and the poor is growing.

THE MARKET ECONOMY

The economy of the United States is based on free enterprise and the market economy. In this system, the majority of business decisions are made by private companies and individuals rather than by the government. The lack of government regulations on businesses gives them greater flexibility than in many other countries and encourages the growth of both businesses and the wider economy. But, the market economy does not cover all aspects of life in the United States. Most people are happy for the government to oversee areas such as education and national defense. The government also regulates, for example, food standards in shops and restaurants.

? Did You Know?

The biggest and most powerful companies in the United States have revenues many times larger than the poorest countries of the world. In 2003, for example, Wal-Mart had revenues of U.S.$258 billion, and General Motors brought in U.S.$195 billion. The GNP of Somalia was only U.S.$1.2 billion, and Ethiopia's GNP was U.S.$6.68 billion.

► The home of a former cotton picker in Tehula, Mississippi, shows the living conditions of some of the poorest people in the United States.

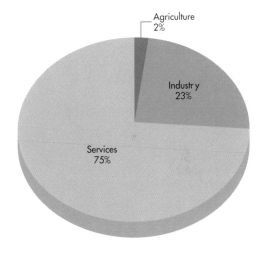

◀ A combine harvester is used to harvest wheat on the Great Plains, near Casselton, North Dakota. The United States is the world's largest exporter of wheat.

AGRICULTURE

Agricultural activity in the United States occupies almost 20 percent of the country's total land area. This highly efficient industry had sales worth over U.S.$200 billion at the last agricultural census in 2002. The value of the industry has led to the growth of agribusiness, in which farms are owned and run by companies or groups of investors rather than by farming families. Nearly 74,000 such farms existed in 2002, but this is still a small number compared to the 1.9 million family or individually-run farms. A major trend in American agriculture over the last 70 years has been a reduction in the total number of farms but an increase in their average size. In 1940, there were about six million farms with an average size of 166 acres (67 hectares), but today there are about two million farms and the average size has increased to 470 acres (190 hectares).

The main crops grown in the United States are soy beans, corn, wheat, cotton, and sorghum. Meat products, especially beef, pork, and poultry, are important. Together with dairy products such as eggs and milk, meat products account for 52.5 percent of all agricultural sales.

Agriculture 2%
Industry 23%
Services 75%

▲ Contribution by sector to national income

Economic Data

- Gross National Income (GNI) in U.S.$: 12.15 trillion
- World rank by GNI: 1
- GNI per capita in U.S.$: 41,400
- World rank by GNI per capita: 5
- Economic growth: 3%

Source: World Bank

OLD AND NEW INDUSTRIES

Industries that developed in the United States in the 19th century, such as steel production, are in decline, mainly due to competition from abroad, where products can be made more cheaply. Many of the country's older, heavier industries are located in the east, in cities such as Pittsburgh, Pennsylvania, where there have been huge job losses. Pittsburgh is now developing high-tech industries such as computer software production in order to generate more work. The people who were employed in older industries, however, often do not have the skills needed for these new jobs.

In the first eight months of 2005, car companies cut 37,000 jobs in the United States in response to a worldwide overproduction of cars. The country's textile industry also lost 46,000 jobs when U.S. firms moved their production overseas to less economically developed countries such as the Philippines where labor costs are much cheaper. During the same period, over 500,000 new jobs were created in the service sector in the United States, many in tourism and retail. Critics point out that most of the new jobs are not equal to the lost jobs in pay and use of workers' skills.

Focus on: Silicon Valley

Silicon Valley is the name of an area located just south of San Francisco, California, where many high-tech firms—such as Intel, Apple, and Hewlett-Packard—are located. High-tech industries began to develop in this area in the 1950s, when Stanford University, in San Francisco, leased land to companies such as Varian Associates. Strong links were formed between the companies and Stanford's research departments, attracting more companies to the area. California's warm climate and pleasant living conditions continue to attract graduates from all over the world to work in Silicon Valley's cutting-edge industries.

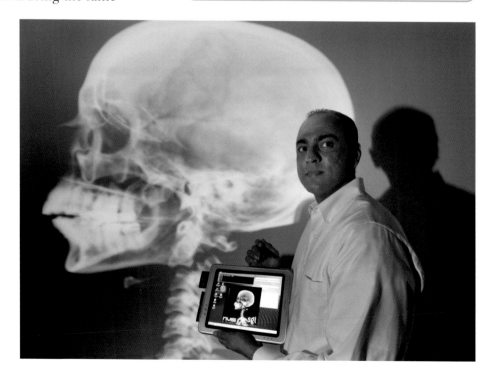

▶ Afshad Mistri of Silicon Graphics demonstrates modern technology that uses special X-ray equipment to create a detailed cross-section of a body part. Many U.S. companies lead the world in such cutting-edge research and development.

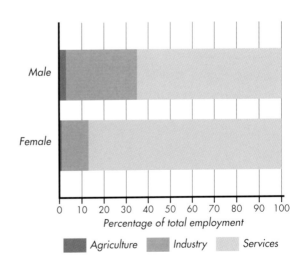

◀ Protesters hold up signs during an unemployment protest in Tempe, Arizona, in 2004. The protest drew attention to the economic policies of President George W. Bush.

UNEMPLOYMENT

In 2005, the United States had 8 million unemployed people, or 5 percent of the population. Several southern states had higher than average unemployment rates, but some northern states where older industries are in decline also had high rates. Michigan, for example, which is a center of the car industry, had 7 percent unemployment. Hawaii, where there are many jobs in the tourist industry, had the lowest unemployment rate, at 2.7 percent.

WEALTH AND POVERTY

In 2004, 12.7 percent of people in the United States were living below the federal poverty line, which in 2003 was estimated to be U.S.$26 a day per person. The distribution of poverty among different races is uneven. Over 25 percent of African Americans and 20 percent of Hispanics live in poverty, compared to just 9 percent of white Americans. In 2004, the average annual income per person in the United States was U.S.$32,937. However,

in Mississippi, which has the highest percentage of African Americans of any state in the United States, the average annual income was over U.S.$8,000 lower.

▲ Labor force by sector and gender

CHAPTER 8

Global Connections

The United States has great influence through its foreign policies, military actions, foreign trade relations, and the exporting of globally recognized brands. At the same time, it is influenced by the commerce, politics, and culture of the rest of the world.

GLOBALIZATION OR AMERICANIZATION?

American transnational companies (TNCs) are responsible for the increasing globalization of the economy. They locate factories or services in different countries for cheap labor or materials— and also to market their products around the world.

Many American TNCs have been very successful, with the names and symbols of brands such as Coca-Cola, Nike, McDonald's, Levi's, Apple, and Microsoft known around the world. Some U.S. firms are so successful at marketing their products worldwide that some people talk about them as

causing Americanization rather than globalization. Although this is good for many U.S. companies, some of them have been criticized for pushing out local businesses in other countries. For example, U.S. media companies export American television shows and movies around the world. In Mexico, the local film industry has all but disappeared because of the popularity of Hollywood movies.

► A film crew on location in Los Angeles, where the movie industry is an important part of the city's economy. Hollywood movies are popular around the whole world.

While the United States has great economic and cultural influence around the world, other countries also influence it. Some well-known American firms, such as Amoco and Miller Brewing, are now owned by foreign companies. Car brands such as Toyota, Honda, and BMW are popular in the United States. Electronics made by Sony and Samsung are available throughout the country, and European and Asian fashions are followed by many Americans. Trends such as Japanese *manga* (comics) and *anime* (animation) are popular among teenagers. Music and movies from around the world are enjoyed by many Americans, and many American universities benefit from international students and visiting faculty. In sports, soccer is a major sport for an increasing number of Americans.

Probably the most important global connection that the United States has is its own people. Many immigrants and their descendants bring food, art, and traditions from around the world to American neighborhoods.

 Did You Know?

The U.S. women's soccer team is one of the top three in world rankings.

Focus on: Rock 'n' Roll

In the 1950s, American musicians influenced by musical styles such as gospel, blues, and country began playing a new style—rock 'n' roll. Their music became popular both in the United States and in Britain. In the 1960s, British rock groups such the Beatles and the Rolling Stones became popular in the United States and immediately began influencing American musicians.

FOREIGN TRADE

The United States' main trading partners are Canada and Mexico. Canada accounts for 19.4 percent of its total trade in goods, and Mexico accounts for 11.3 percent. Together, the three countries form a free-trade area established by the North American Free Trade Agreement, or NAFTA. NAFTA, which took effect at the beginning of 1994, aims to reduce trade barriers between its three members and to create a trading group that can better compete with other trading groups, such as the European Union (EU).

▼ A Toyota technician shows an emergency medical technician (EMT) how to disable the electronic motor of a Toyota Prius in case of a problem.

▲ Containers of imported goods are unloaded at Long Beach, California.

IMPORTS AND EXPORTS

After Canada, the second biggest exporter to the United States is China. In 2004, the United States imported U.S.$196.7 billion of goods from China, while it exported U.S.$34.7 billion to China. This is known as a trade deficit. In fact, the United States has an overall trade deficit, and in December 2005, it imported U.S.$68.9 billion worth of goods more than it exported. The United States mainly imports oil, electrical goods, and textiles, as well as some foods. Apart from wheat, the United States is an important exporter of minerals, processed foods and drinks, vehicles and vehicle components, airplanes, technology, and financial services.

Did You Know?

Through the United States Agency for International Development (USAID), the United States gives financial help to over 100 countries around the world.

INTERNATIONAL ROLES

As the world's only superpower, the United States plays a major role in many of the bodies that are involved in international affairs. The G8 is a group of eight major developed countries, including the United States, that meets annually to discuss economic and political issues. In 2005, the group met at Gleneagles in Scotland where two of the main issues were development in Africa and climate change. The United States has only recently come into line with other countries and accepted that climate change is occurring as a result of human activities.

As a founding member of the United Nations (UN), the United States is influential in UN affairs. The UN tries to resolve conflicts by encouraging negotiation and disarmament, and sending peacekeeping troops to the world's trouble spots. Some UN member countries, including France and Russia, did not support the U.S.-led invasion of Iraq in 2003, which was undertaken without full authorization by the UN Security Council. In 2002, North Korea claimed that it had nuclear weapons and was developing nuclear reactors. The following year North Korea withdrew from the Nuclear Non-proliferation Treaty, the international treaty that controls the spread of nuclear weapons. The United States, along with countries such as China, has been instrumental in trying to resolve this issue. In September 2005, North Korea re-signed the treaty and agreed to give up its nuclear activities.

◀ World leaders at the G8 Summit at Gleneagles, Scotland, July 2005. U.S. president George W. Bush stands in the front row, second from the left. British prime minister Tony Blair stands at the podium. The United States and Britain are close allies.

Focus on: NATO

The North Atlantic Treaty Organization (NATO) is an alliance of 26 countries, including the United States, Canada, and many countries of Europe. NATO was set up after the end of World War II in order to safeguard the freedom and security of its members by political or military means. Countries in NATO agree that an armed attack or threat to one of its members is regarded as an attack or threat against all of its members and pledge to respond as a unit. The United States is the largest country in this organization and, arguably, the most powerful. Supporters of NATO suggest that this European-American alliance helps to maintain world peace because it includes a large proportion of the countries of the economically developed world and that these countries together makes up an extremely powerful force that no one would want to fight.

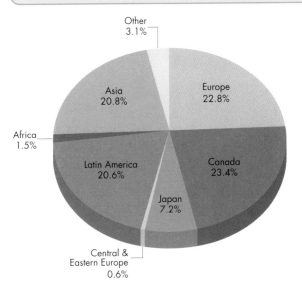

▲ Destination of exports by major trading region

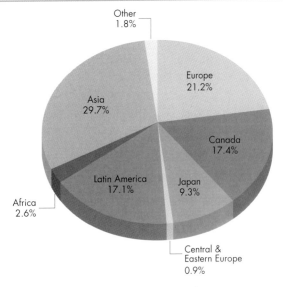

▲ Origin of imports by major trading region

CHAPTER 9

Transportation and Communications

The huge size of the United States has led to the development of an extensive transport infrastructure that includes roads, railways, airports, and ports. This infrastructure makes it possible for people to travel from place to place easily and move goods efficiently over long distances. The distance between New York and Los Angeles—2,462 miles (3,961 km)—is about the same as the distance from London to the North Pole. Many people in the United States choose to fly between cities rather than take several days or weeks to travel across the country by road or rail.

ROAD AND RAIL

In the 19th century, the construction of railroads helped to open up the west of the country by making transportation to these distant areas accessible to all. Today, the railroads are much more important for carrying freight, such as wheat or iron ore. Road transportation, however, still carries the majority of freight because railroads provide only limited access to many parts of the country. The country has nearly 4 million miles (over 6 million km) of road, which trucks share with over 140 million cars. For trips over 50 miles, 90 percent of Americans use cars and only 1 percent take trains. With over one-third of American households having two cars and one-quarter having at least three, gasoline consumption is high. Many experts see car use as the cause of environmental problems such as air pollution. Traffic congestion is a problem in many cities.

Did You Know?

The first electric traffic lights may have been invented by a Salt Lake City, Utah, policeman in 1912. Manually controlled traffic lights were installed in Cleveland, Ohio, in 1914. Automatic traffic lights may have been invented in 1917.

◀ A driver on a Greyhound bus in Washington, D. C. Greyhound bus routes link many U.S. cities. After the terrorist attacks in 2001, the buses were fitted with new safety devices, including a gate (left) to protect the driver from attacks by passengers.

AIR TRAVEL

The United States has 5,128 public-use airports, and the nation has the largest number of airports and air connections in the world. Many of these flights are internal domestic flights between the country's big cities. The busiest U.S. airport in 2004 was Hartsfield Airport in Atlanta, Georgia, which had over 83 million passengers.

Focus on: Bay Area Rapid Transit (BART)

San Francisco, California, has a population of over 740,000 people. The city suffers from air pollution caused by car exhaust. In 1974, BART was opened. It is an electric railway that travels above and below ground, transporting people between the suburbs and the city, and reducing the amount of car use and air pollution. Travel times are much faster by BART than by car, but the city is still having problems in encouraging more people to use this efficient system.

Transport & Communications Data

- Total roads: 3,972,985 miles/6,393,603 km
- Total paved roads: 2,597,485 miles/ 4,180,053 km
- Total unpaved roads: 1,375,500 miles/ 2,213,550 km
- Total railways: 141,515 miles/227,736 km
- Major airports: 5,120
- Cars per 1,000 people: 481
- Mobile phones per 1,000 people: 543
- Personal computers per 1,000 people: 659
- Internet users per 1,000 people: 551

Source: World Bank and CIA World Factbook

▲ One of the 38 cable cars that run along three routes in San Francisco, California. This old-fashioned transportation system is used mainly by tourists.

 Did You Know?

The famous cable cars that ride up and down the hills of San Francisco, carrying thousands of tourists a week between the city center and Fisherman's Wharf, are designated historical monuments.

WATER NETWORKS

The United States has 25,483 miles (41,009 km) of waterways, and some of these routes are very important for trade. This is especially true of the Mississippi River which, with its tributaries and the Missouri River, provides a water route out of the Great Lakes region down to the Gulf ports in the south. Corn, wheat, and soy beans are transported down the river on large barges. Although slow, this form of transport is ideal for bulky, low-value goods because it is cheaper than transporting them by road. The United States' most important port is South Louisiana, on the coast of the Gulf of Mexico. In 2004, 238 million tons (216 million metric tons) of goods moved through this port.

▼ Barges on the Mississippi River near Baton Rouge, Louisiana. Huge loads can be transported on these barges, which are towed by tugboats.

MEDIA & COMMUNICATIONS

The media plays a major role in the everyday lives of most Americans, and there are over 13,000 radio stations, over 1,700 television stations, and about 9,000 cable networks. The Public Broadcasting Service (PBS) and National Public Radio (NPR) are run with the help of

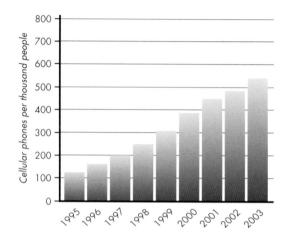

▲ Cellular phone use, 1995–2003

government funding, but all other channels are privately operated. There are more than 181 million telephone lines, more than 160 million cell phones (mobile phones), and about 163 million Internet users. U.S. companies dominate the software needed for accessing the Internet, and a few large companies, such as AOL Time Warner, Disney, and Viacom, control large shares of the U.S. media.

Although most Americans say television is their most reliable source of information, there are nevertheless more than 1,500 daily newspapers. Many of these cover mainly local issues, while famous papers such as the *Washington Post* and the *New York Times* give in-depth coverage of national and international news. One strength of the United States is its emphasis of freedom of speech and freedom of the press, both of which are protected by the Constitution. Americans have the right to express their opinions in the media—even when they disagree with the government—without fear of prosecution.

Focus on: The Development of the Internet

The Internet originated as a way of sharing information between a number of computer networks in different locations. At first, it was only used by the U.S. military and the federal government. The idea was further developed in the 1960s by research scientists at the Massachusetts Institute of Technology (MIT), who realized its potential for the transmission of knowledge. By the early 1970s, the first email program was written, and the term "Internet" began to be used. Private companies such as AOL became involved in the 1980s, and the Internet quickly developed into a technology used throughout the United States—and the world.

▼ Access to computers has become increasingly important in education. In this new school in Vail, Arizona, all students are supplied with Apple iBook laptops.

CHAPTER 10

Education and Health

The United States has well-developed education and health-care systems, but access to these services is not equal for all people.

SCHOOLS

Although the country has a federal Department of Education, most funding and supervision of education is under the control of individual states. The level of funding through local taxes is, therefore, a reflection of the wealth of a particular area, resulting in some areas being better provided for than others. Literacy rates are high, at 99 percent for the whole country, but standards of literacy vary, and low levels of literacy and numeracy are problems for many adults at work or in seeking work. In 2002, the

Did You Know?

In 2003, 60 percent of all American 3- and 4-year-olds—about five million children—were enrolled in preschool programs.

U.S. government passed the No Child Left Behind Act to improve standards in schools and encourage early reading and proficiency in math. State and workplace programs address problems of adult literacy.

All children in the United States receive at least 11 years of education, for which no fees are charged. Only 10 percent of schools are private, and most of these are linked to religious foundations. Most students attend elementary school, followed by middle school (called junior high school in some places), and then high school. Students may leave school at the age of 16, although very few do because it is difficult to get a job without having graduated from high school. Most American students graduate from high school at about the age of 18.

High-school graduation rates vary between states. Many of those with low graduation rates are southern states, such as Louisiana, Alabama,

◀ Graduating from high school is an important moment in the lives of many young Americans, and it is often marked by ceremonies and parties. These students are celebrating at Stuart High, in Falls Church, Virginia.

and Arkansas. This may be because finishing high school is not seen as a priority in some communities. In 2001, 88 percent of high-school seniors graduated. Overall figures show that 93 percent of white students, 87 percent of black students, and 63 percent of Hispanic students completed high school.

HIGHER EDUCATION

Over half of high-school graduates in the United States go on to higher education. In 2003, this was more than 16 million students. Higher education in the country is expensive, however, and the majority of students combine their studies with jobs. Even if they work, many students graduate from college with debts of around U.S.$40,000,

which may take them many years to pay back. Higher education is available at local community colleges, at which a student can earn an associate's degree after two years of study. Bachelor's degrees at state and private colleges and universities take about four years. Some students continue on to earn master's degrees, Ph.D.s, and various advanced degrees in medicine, law, and business.

 Did You Know?

Of the 182.2 million people in the United States over age 25 in 2000, 80 percent had a high school diploma. Nearly 22 percent had a college degree, and nearly 9 percent had a postgraduate degree.

Focus on: The Ivy League Universities

The Ivy League universities are among the most prestigious universities in the United States. Many people think the name "Ivy League" comes from the ivy-covered walls of their buildings. The Ivy League, however, was founded as a sports league. Today, these universities are renowned for high academic standards and for difficulty of gaining admission. The eight Ivy League members are Harvard University, Yale University, Columbia University, University of Pennsylvania, Princeton University, Dartmouth College, Brown University, and Cornell University.

▲ Students on the campus of Columbia University, which was founded in 1754 as King's College.

HEALTH CARE FOR THE MAJORITY

Most health care in the United States is privately funded, and people are usually responsible for paying for their own health care. Many people either buy their own health insurance or receive health insurance as a benefit from an employer. Health insurance is often offered as an incentive to attract a new employee to a job and will usually cover the employee's family. Having health insurance is important to most Americans because treatment for a serious illness is very expensive in the United States: all aspects of health care have to be paid for—including the hospital room, the services of doctors and nurses, food, medicine, and tests.

 Did You Know?

As the nation has become wealthier, levels of obesity have increased in children. Between 1976 and 1980, only 6 percent of children were obese. By 2002, this statistic had risen to 16 percent.

The cost of health care in the United States has led many Americans to be interested in preventative health care, and many Americans are very concerned with health and fitness. Taking vitamins and other supplements are also popular ways to improve well-being.

UNEVEN ACCESS

The United States has a government-run health insurance program for all people over the age of 65. For people with low incomes, the United States has a government health-care program called Medicaid, which provides some health insurance for 38 million people, as well as long-term care for 12 million elderly and disabled people. Although 75 percent of people receiving Medicaid are parents and children from low-income families, 70 percent of the program's funding is spent on the elderly. However, in 2004, the United States also had 45.8 million people who were neither insured nor eligible to receive Medicaid—nearly 16 percent of the country's population. As the cost of health care in the United States continues to rise and the number of people without health insurance also grows, some people are concerned that planned government cuts to the Medicaid program will affect the most vulnerable people in U.S. society.

◀ A medical team reviews a patient's progress at the Hackensack Medical Center, in New Jersey.

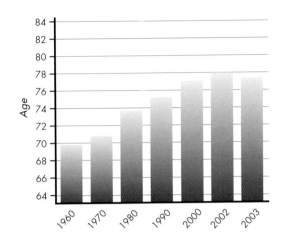

▲ Life expectancy at birth, 1960–2003

(Chart y-axis labeled "Age" ranging from 64 to 84; x-axis years: 1960, 1970, 1980, 1990, 2000, 2002, 2003)

Education and Health Data

- Life expectancy at birth male: 74.9
- Life expectancy at birth female: 80
- Infant mortality rate per 1,000: 7
- Under five mortality rate per 1,000: 8
- Physicians per 1,000 people: 5.5
- Health expenditure as % of GDP: 14.6%
- Education expenditure as % of GDP: 5.7%
- Primary school net enrollment: 93%
- Student-teacher ratio, primary school: 14.8
- Adult literacy as % age 15+: 99%

Source: United Nations Agencies and World Bank

Focus on: Obesity in the United States

One of the most pressing health problems in the United States is obesity and complications of obesity, such as diabetes. Over 65 percent of the U.S. population is overweight, and 31 percent is classed as obese. Among the reasons for such a high level of obesity are a diet that includes a lot of cheap fast food, which is high in calories and saturated fats, and also the fact that many Americans are increasingly dependent on cars and unwilling to exercise regularly. It is thought that the rise in obesity in the country will lead to an increase in the number of cases of diabetes, heart disease, breathing problems, cancer, and serious joint problems. Each year 300,000 people in the United States die prematurely as a result of being overweight.

◄ A fitness instructor leads an exercise class in Linden, New Jersey.

CHAPTER 11

Culture and Religion

The United States has often been referred to as a "melting pot" of many different peoples and cultures. Since the birth of the country, the influx of immigrants from all over the world has resulted in a rich combination of ideas and traditions that has given the United States its own unique culture. For example, music brought by early French settlers in Louisiana contributed to the development of Cajun music. The African slaves who came to the United States brought with them the sounds and rhythms of their native music, which contributed to the development of blues, jazz, rock 'n' roll, R & B, and hip-hop.

Some festivals celebrated in the United States are purely American. Almost all Americans celebrate Thanksgiving and Independence Day, which is on July 4, and marks the signing of the Declaration of Independence. Others relate to the many cultures that make up the population.

Focus on: Jazz

Jazz music is one of America's most distinctive cultural creations. The music developed in part from the rhythms and musical heritage that black slaves brought with them from Africa. Early in the history of jazz, New Orleans was the center of the jazz community. By the 1930s, jazz was played and enjoyed by both blacks and whites. Some of the greatest jazz musicians include Charlie Parker, Miles Davis, John Coltrane, and Thelonious Monk.

◀ Bagpipe players from the U.S. Marine Corps march past St. Patrick's Cathedral during the March 17, 2001, St. Patrick's Day Parade in New York City. The St. Patrick's Day Parade is a popular annual event in New York City.

St. Patrick's Day parades are held in cities with many Irish-Americans, such as Boston and New York City. The Calle Oche Festival, which celebrates Hispanic culture, is held every March in Miami, Florida, and is said to be the largest street party in the world. During summers, Milwaukee, Wisconsin, holds a different ethnic festival nearly each week.

NATIVE AMERICAN CULTURE

Native Americans make up only 1 percent of the population of the United States, but many Native Americans are determined to maintain their ancient cultures and ways of life. Several of the larger Native American groups organize regular gatherings, or pow-wows, in order to celebrate Native American music, dance, and crafts and to study their history. Today, the largest Native American group is the Navajo. Members of the Navajo live in their own nation, which spreads across parts of Utah, New Mexico, and Arizona, and they have their own elected government. Although they live under most of the same laws as other American citizens, the Navajo have their own police and schools; set their own taxes; and speak their own language, combining modern life with their rich cultural heritage.

▼ A pow-wow in Cashmere, Washington, offers members of different Native American groups the chance to celebrate their cultures and traditions.

RELIGION AND THE STATE

The United States has no state religion, and the Constitution allows citizens the freedom to worship (or not worship) as they please. While many American children in public schools say the Pledge of Allegiance, which mentions God, there are no religious ceremonies during the school day.

▼ Members of a congregation leave a Baptist church in Beaufort, South Carolina, after a service. Baptists are a major Christian denomination in the United States, especially in the southern states.

In 2002, over 84 percent of Americans identified themselves as Christians, whether they were affiliated with, or members of, a particular church. Reflecting the religious beliefs of many of the early European settlers, Protestants make up about 52 percent of American Christians, while Roman Catholics make up about 24 percent. Baptists form the largest group within the Protestant church and are particularly numerous in the southern states, which are often known as the Bible Belt. Churches play a major role in many communities, both as places of worship and as centers for social life. The United States is also home to about 6 million Jews—the largest Jewish population outside of Israel. The greatest concentration of American Jews is in New York, though many also live in Florida, California, and Illinois.

One of the fastest-growing religions in the United States is Islam. Most of this growth has been in the African American community, which now makes up about 42 percent of American Muslims. There are over 1,000 mosques in the country, with the vast majority of them in metropolitan areas.

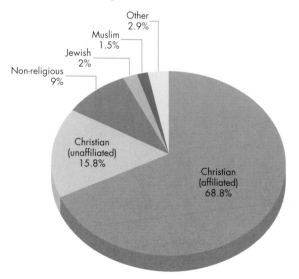

▲ Major religions of the United States

In 2001, nearly 26 million Americans (9 percent) said they were not affiliated with any religion—an increase of 6 percent since 1990. Increasing numbers of Americans are looking for alternatives to traditional religions that may answer their questions. Some of the beliefs to which they are turning—including pagan religions and Eastern religions such as Buddhism—have ancient roots.

NEW RELIGIONS

During the 19th century, several new religious groups were created in the United States. Two of the better-known of these groups are the Mormons, who are members of the Church of Latter Day Saints, and the Jehovah's Witnesses. Both of these groups are Christian, and both of them have spread worldwide from their beginnings in the United States. The Mormons were founded by Joseph Smith, and their beliefs are based on the *Book of Mormon* which Smith reported had been revealed to him. Mormons eventually moved west to avoid persecution and settled in Utah, in what is now Salt Lake City, the present-day location of their headquarters. It is estimated that the United States has over 3 million Mormons. Jehovah's Witnesses believe in the imminent return of Jesus Christ, and they are known for preaching this belief door-to-door. The United States has nearly 2 million Jehovah's Witnesses.

▼ Dr. Amina Wadud leads a group of women during the first public, mixed-gender Muslim prayer service, held in New York City in March 2005.

CHAPTER 12

Leisure and Tourism

The average American works hard for a living, spending more hours at work and having less vacation time than the average European. Because of this, leisure time is especially valued in the United States. It is common, for example, for families to go camping for just a couple of days over a weekend so that they can spend time together. Taking such short vacations, it is difficult to travel long distances. This may explain why it is estimated that only 20 percent of the U.S. population has a passport for travel abroad. Another reason may be that the United States has so many vacation destinations within its borders, with a huge choice ranging from long, sandy beaches and the scenery of its deserts and mountains to historic and vibrant cities such as New York and San Francisco.

THE TOURISM INDUSTRY

The tourism industry in the United States is worth U.S.$99 billion and is, therefore, very important to the country's economy. There are about 2.6 million hotel rooms rented every day in the United States, supporting hundreds of thousands of jobs. In addition to supporting the people who work in the tourism industry, revenue from tourism is also important to the United States because it contributes to public spending through the tax tourists pay on goods and services. If the tourism industry were to collapse, it is estimated that each American household would need to pay around U.S.$898 in taxes to prevent public budgets from falling.

▼ A family enjoys a wilderness camping expedition in the Sawtooth National Forest, in Idaho.

With most American employees having only two weeks of vacation a year, the vast majority of people vacation within the United States, often within their own state. Outdoor vacations are popular. In the winter, the many ski resorts in the Rocky Mountains and elsewhere are popular, and the warm climate of Florida attracts visitors to its beaches all year round. Many families visit attractions such as Disneyland, near Los Angeles, and Disneyworld, in Florida. When Americans do travel abroad, the most popular destination for them to visit is Western Europe (40 percent of all overseas travel), and the most-visited country is Britain (14 percent of all overseas travel).

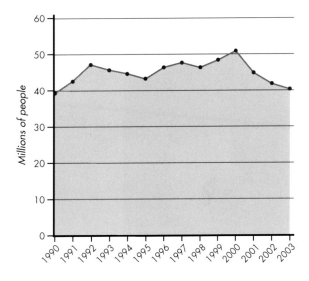

▲ Changes in international tourism, 1990–2003

Focus on: Las Vegas

Las Vegas lies in the middle of the desert in Nevada. The city celebrated its one-hundredth birthday in 2005. In its short history, Las Vegas has become the gambling capital of the world. In 2004, it attracted over 37 million visitors. The huge casino resorts that line the Strip (the city's main thoroughfare) feature 24-hour gambling tables and slot machines, as well as restaurants, high-class shopping, and extravagant shows. So much money is earned by the city in its casinos that Nevada has no state income tax.

 Did You Know?

The tourism industry in the United States employs approximately 7.3 million people.

◀ A killer whale performs for an audience at SeaWorld Adventure Park, one of several theme parks located around Orlando, Florida.

▲ Skiers enjoy the snow at the Deer Valley Ski Resort, in Utah.

VISITORS TO THE UNITED STATES

In 2003, over 40 million overseas visitors came to the United States. The three states that received the most overseas visitors were New York, Florida, and California. New York City is the country's top all-year-round tourist destination, offering world-famous sights such as the Statue of Liberty, the Empire State Building, and Central Park, as well as many internationally known museums, theaters, and art galleries. Both federal and state governments invest money in marketing the United States as a holiday destination because of the importance of creating and maintaining a wide range of jobs.

 Did You Know?

In-line skates were developed in the 1980s by two American ice-hockey players who were looking for a way to continue practicing their skating technique even when there was no ice.

LEISURE

Over 95 percent of people in the United States spend an average of five hours a day on sport or leisure, with watching television accounting for about three hours per day. Other popular activities include shopping—a visit to the local mall is often a social activity—as well as a wide range of hobbies and cultural activities such as going to movies, exhibits, or concerts.

SPORTS

The United States is a great sporting nation. In the Summer Olympics of 2004, the United States was the most successful team, winning over 100 medals, of which 35 were gold. Sports, including football, basketball, and baseball, are played in schools and communities and are watched by many spectators. If a student is successful in high-school sports, it is possible for him or her to win a scholarship to play for a university team while studying for a degree. Many people also play sports just for fun.

Tourism in the United States

- Tourist arrivals, millions: 40.356
- Earnings from tourism in U.S.$: 99,815,997,440
- Tourism as % foreign earnings: 10%
- Tourist departures, millions: 54.206
- Expenditure on tourism in U.S.$: 80,621,002,752

Source: World Bank

THE BIG LEAGUES

Professional sports of all types are popular in the United States, and a wide variety of sporting events are televised. Many Americans enjoy watching their favorite athletes and teams compete. Major League Baseball teams compete each year to see which team will win the World Series. The National Football League season ends with the Super Bowl, a championship game that is often the most-watched sporting event of the year in the country. The teams of the National Basketball Association (NBA) are also enormously popular. National Hockey League (NHL) teams compete each year for the Stanley Cup.

Car racing has large numbers of fans in the United States, particularly stock car racing, which is popular as a spectator sport. The National Association for Stock Car Auto Racing (NASCAR) oversees the sport. The United States also hosts several important international sporting events, including major golf and tennis tournaments and the U.S. Open (tennis). Soccer is also increasingly popular.

 Did You Ynow?

In the 1970s, an East-coast surfer developed the first board for use on snow. Snowboarding became popular in the late 1980s, and it became an Olympic sport in 1998.

Focus on: Baseball

Many people think of baseball as the national pastime of the United States. Baseball developed from the English game of rounders and other games. American children play baseball in Little League, and most parks in the United States have at least one baseball field. The first professional baseball league was founded in 1871. By 2006, Major League Baseball had 30 teams, active minor leagues, and a long season that runs from April to October. No baseball team has been more successful than the New York Yankees; by 2004, the Yankees had won the World Series 26 times.

▼ A sell-out crowd watches a football game between the New York Jets and the Indianapolis Colts at Giants Stadium, in New Jersey.

CHAPTER 13

Environment and Conservation

The high level of economic development of the United States has come at some cost to its environment. Although there is great understanding in the United States of the impact of human activities on natural environments, many areas in the country are still under pressure from resource extraction or misuse. In 1892, the influential Sierra Club was created in California by John Muir to encourage the protection of the wild spaces in the United States. The Sierra Club helped to set up the country's first national parks, and it continues to play an important role in raising awareness of human impacts on natural surroundings. Newer pressure groups such as Friends of the Earth and Greenpeace began in the United States during the second half of the 20th century and have worked to highlight what they see as gross misuse of resources and land.

SOIL EROSION

Intensive agriculture, especially in the Midwest, has led to some areas of soil being plowed and left unvegetated. During times of heavy rainfall in these areas, exposed topsoil is washed away, gradually reducing the fertility of the land. Farmers have addressed this problem through the use of chemical fertilizers, but excessive use of these fertilizers has itself made the soil more crumbly and prone to removal by wind, making the problem worse.

AIR POLLUTION AND ACID RAIN

Although the overall air quality of the United States has improved over the last 30 years, air quality in U.S. cities such as Los Angeles is still getting worse as a result of pollutants from vehicle exhausts. Problems with air quality have led to a rise in the numbers of breathing problems in the U.S. population and cause 159,000 trips to hospital emergency rooms and over 6 million asthma attacks each summer. The parts of the United States with the worst air-pollution problems are Los Angeles; the

◀ Los Angeles is often shrouded in smog that is caused by the exhaust of the millions of vehicles that travel along its roads.

Houston-Galveston area, in the south; and the heavily urbanized northeast.

Emissions from cars and factories produce sulphur dioxide and nitrogen dioxide which, when dissolved in rainfall, cause acid rain. Acid rain affects the ability of trees to absorb nutrients through their roots and to photosynthesize efficiently. The leaves of affected trees turn yellow, and the trees may eventually die. The pollutants are often carried by the wind away from the areas in which they are produced and fall in rain in a distant area. In the northeastern United States, for example the Green Mountains, in Vermont, are affected by acid rain. The acid-rain problem also crosses the United States-Canada border. In 1991, Canada and the United States signed the Air Quality Agreement to reduce levels of acid rain by using filters on factory and power station chimneys. Since then, there has been reduction in emissions of over one-third.

Environmental and Conservation Data

- Forested area as % total land area: 27%
- Protected area as % total land area: 15.8%
- Number of protected areas: 7,748

SPECIES DIVERSITY

Category	Known species	Threatened species
Mammals	428	37
Breeding birds	508	55
Reptiles	360	27
Amphibians	283	25
Fish	1,101	130
Plants	19,473	169

Source: World Resources Institute

▼ The forests on Mount Mitchell, in North Carolina, show evidence of acid-rain damage, with branches stripped of foliage and some dead trees.

PROTECTING THE NATURAL HERITAGE

Much of the natural environment of the United States has some protection at either local, state, or national levels. Included at the national level are parks, seashores, rivers, and lake shores.

The country has 52 national parks, which are run by the National Parks Service. These parks cover landscapes as varied as the Rocky Mountains, desert areas of the southwest, and tundra regions in Alaska. Their goal is both to protect the environment of the parks and, at the same time, allow visitors to enjoy the parks' natural beauty. The first national park was Yellowstone, in Wyoming, which was set up

in 1872 to protect its volcanic landscape. People still come from around the world to view its geysers and boiling pools. Like Grand Canyon National Park, Yellowstone attracts over 4 million visitors a year. Other national parks include the arctic tundra of Alaska's Denali National Park; the rocky coastline and forest of Maine's Acadia National Park; Utah's dramatic Canyonlands National Park in Utah; and the swamplands of Florida's Everglades.

▼ Wilderness areas in national parks are vital to protecting both habitats and species such as this mountain lion, which was photographed in Canyonlands National Park, in Utah.

 Did You Know?

Ninety percent of the wood in New Orleans' historic French Quarter is infested with the Formosan termite, an alien species, and millions of dollars are spent in pest control every year. The termites arrived 60 years ago, in the wood of packing crates from Southeast Asia.

THE ARCTIC NATIONAL WILDLIFE REFUGE

The Arctic National Wildlife Refuge, which is located in the United States near its border with Canada, is an important area for caribou, or reindeer. It is an isolated area, and its wildlife thrives away from human interference. However, its protection is now in doubt because of pressure for oil and gas exploration in the refuge. Environmentalists fear that drilling in the refuge will interfere with the breeding and migration of caribou herds and damage the fragile ecosystems of the tundra for many years to come. Environmentalists argue that Americans should aim to reduce their fossil-fuel use before exploiting such unique and fragile areas.

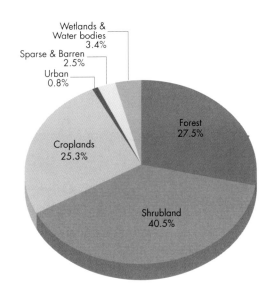

▲ Habitat type as percentage of total area

Focus on: Alien Invaders

It is estimated that about 6,000 alien, or non-native, plant and animal species have entered the United States as a result of human activity. These alien species often cause problems because they do not have any natural predators in their new homes. The tamarisk is an alien tree that was introduced to the United States from Europe in the 19th century as an ornamental plant. It has spread from the parks where it was originally planted to riverbanks, especially in the southwest, where it shades out the native cottonwoods and willows. The tamarisk has reduced the habitat for native birds and animals and changed the ecosystem. In order to help reduce the problem, weekend volunteers go out "tammy bashing," or pulling up young tamarisks.

◀ Children from the city of Miami, Florida, learn about wildlife from a ranger in Everglades National Park.

CHAPTER 14

Future Challenges

The United States is an immensely wealthy and powerful nation, but it has a number of problems that it must face during the 21st century as both its economy and position in world politics change.

INTERNATIONAL RELATIONS

Since the terrorist attacks in September 11, 2001, the United States has taken a strong stand against countries it perceives as threats. This has increased tensions between the United States and countries such as Iran, which has long been hostile to the United States. U.S. relations with many Muslim and Arab nations are strained because of U.S. presence in the Middle East, particularly in Iraq. Another source of tension between the United States and the Muslim countries of the Middle East is the continuing support the United States gives to Israel, although the United States has played a major role in pushing forward the peace process between Israel and the Palestinians. The United States is also involved in countering the potential nuclear threat posed by countries such as North Korea and Iran.

Preventing terrorism will continue to be a challenge for the United States. In 2002, as a result of the terrorist attacks of the previous year, the U.S. government created the Department of Homeland Security, which is charged with protecting the country's people and property from harm. The first major challenge to the new department, however, came not from terrorism but from Hurricane Katrina, and showed that the United States needs to improve its ability to respond to catastrophic events.

U.S. involvement in conflicts in other countries is having an impact on the country's economy. In 2004, U.S.\$370.7 billion was spent on the country's military, and some people have questioned whether continuing this much military spending is viable. In the future, the

◀ Young Americans from diverse ethnic backgrounds show pride in their shared national identity.

rise of other world groups, such as a united and expanded Europe, and the fast-growing economies of both China and India may challenge the position of the United States as the world's only superpower.

GROWING DISPARITIES

One of the major challenges for domestic policy in the United States is to address the increasing gap between rich and poor in the country. The United Nations calculates that the wealthiest 10 percent of Americans enjoy 30 percent of the country's wealth, while the poorest 10 percent share less than 2 percent. One way of dealing with this problem is by improving education. Young people who leave school without solid skills are less likely to be able to succeed in higher education, which is required for most high-paying jobs. Jobs in the new high-tech

industries that have great promise of economic growth, for example, require advanced education. Some government programs are being developed to tackle these problems. For example, Reading First is a nationwide program intended to encourage the youngest students to develop good reading skills. It is based on studies that show that students who read well in the early grades are usually more successful in later grades.

Providing more Americans with the skills and opportunities to better contribute to and share in their country's wealth and success—along with continued economic growth—could help to reduce the growing disparities in the country. If more people in the United States were able to earn a good living, crime levels might fall and a more cohesive society might grow.

Focus on: Defense Against Natural Disasters

After the devastating hurricane damage of 2004 and 2005, one important future challenge for the United States is to protect vulnerable land and communities along the country's coasts. The main threats are tidal waves along the Pacific coast and

hurricanes along the coasts of the southeast and the Gulf of Mexico. More than half of the country's population lives on or near a coast. Research into better and faster evacuation of these areas needs to be carried out.

◀ The future of fuel stations? An electric vehicle passes through an alternative fuel station in San Diego, California. At this station, customers can fill up with a variety of fuels, including gasoline and natural gas.

Time Line

c.8000 B.C. Migration of humans from Asia to America across a land bridge.

A.D. c.1000 Viking explorer Leif Erikson reaches North America.

1492 Explorer Christopher Columbus reaches the Bahamas.

1607 First permanent English colony founded at Jamestown, Virginia.

1620 Pilgrim Fathers (Puritans) found Plymouth Colony in Massachusetts.

1733 There are now 13 British colonies.

1763 French and Indian War ends with Britain controlling Canada and all land in North America east of the Mississippi River.

1773 Colonists rebel against being taxed by Britain in the Boston Tea Party.

1776 The Declaration of Independence is signed on July 4.

1781 British surrender at Yorktown, Virginia.

1783 The American Revolution officially ends with the signing of the Treaty of Paris.

1787 Constitution of the United States ratified.

1789 George Washington is elected president of the United States.

1803 Louisiana Purchase.

1861 The Civil War begins.

1865 The Civil War ends; slavery is abolished; President Abraham Lincoln is assassinated.

1867 Alaska purchased from Russia.

1917 The United States enters World War I on the side of the Allies.

1929 Wall Street stock market crash.

1929–1939 The Great Depression

1941 Pearl Harbor is bombed by Japan; the United States enters World War II.

1945 The United States drops atomic bombs on the Japanese cities of Hiroshima and Nagasaki, ending the war in the Pacific.

1945–1989 Cold War with the Soviet Union.

1950–1953 Korean War.

1965 U.S. troops begin fighting in Vietnam war (until 1973).

1973–1974 Oil-crisis as OPEC countries limit oil exports; President Richard Nixon resigns.

1979 Iranian militants take over U.S. embassy and hold 62 American hostages for 444 days.

1980s Period of economic growth.

1990–1991 The United States leads a coalition to liberate Kuwait from Iraq in the Gulf War.

1992 Democratic president Bill Clinton is elected.

1996 President Bill Clinton is re-elected.

1998 Al-Qaeda attacks U.S. embassies in Tanzania and Kenya.

2001 Republican president George W. Bush takes office; al-Qaeda terrorists attack on September 11; the United States attacks Afghanistan in October in order to pursue al-Qaeda leaders.

2003 The United States invades Iraq, removes Saddam Hussein from power, and begins the transition to a new Iraqi government.

2004 President George W. Bush is re-elected.

2005 Hurricane Katrina devastates Louisiana, particularly New Orleans, in September.

Glossary

acid rain rainfall that contains sulphur dioxide and nitrogen oxides from exhaust gases, making it more acidic than normal

agribusiness large-scale, commercial farming

Baptists members of a Christian denomination who believe in adult baptism by immersion in water

census an official gathering of information about a population in a certain area, often carried out at intervals of ten years

civil rights the rights of a citizen to liberty and equality; used in the United States particularly with reference to African Americans' movement to achieve these rights

communism a political system that abolishes private ownership and emphasizes common ownership of property and the means of production

Confederacy the government formed by the seceding southern states during the Civil War

democracy a political system in which government representatives are chosen by the people of a country in free elections

ecosystem a particular area consisting of living organisms (plants, animals, etc.) and the physical environment that surrounds them

emissions waste gases and particles given out from factory chimneys and motor vehicles

federal related to the central government of the United States that unites the states into one country

free enterprise an economic system in which businesses are allowed to be free from state or government control

geothermal related to energy generated by Earth's core that can be tapped by humans via hot rocks or water and can either be used directly or harnessed to generate electricity

globalization the process by which the economies and businesses of various countries become increasingly interrelated

gross national product (GNP) the total value of all goods and services produced annually by a nation

high-tech industries industries that use the latest techniques and technologies, usually referring to telecommunications, electronics, and medicine

Hispanic related to or being a person of Latin American descent living in the United States, especially a person from Central or South America, Puerto Rico, Cuba, or Mexico

hurricane a tropical cyclone that begins out at sea and moves inland with wind speeds exceeding 75 mph (120 km per hour)

levee a barrier that protects against flooding

market economy an economy based on supply and demand, with little or no government control

migrants people who moves away from their original homes or countries

naturalization the process of becoming a citizen of a country

photosynthesis the process by which green plants build up sugars using solar energy, carbon dioxide, and water

photovoltaic using the Sun's energy to create an electric current

prairie the large plain in the center of North America which was originally grassland

stock market a place in which shares of companies are bought and sold

sustainable using resources in a way that preserves them for the future

tectonic plates the large areas of Earth's crust that lie on top of molten rock beneath

tornado a violent, revolving storm that forms a funnel cloud over heated land

trade deficit the difference between the value of a country's imports and exports when it imports more than it exports

transnational companies (TNCs) companies that have their headquarters in one country and their production units in other nations

tributary a river that feeds a larger river

tundra a treeless, high-latitude area in which vegetation consists mostly of grasses, lichens, and mosses

Union the northern free states during the Civil War

urban sprawl uncontrolled spreading of an urban area

Further Information

BOOKS TO READ

Anderson, Dale. *World Almanac Library of the American Revolution*. World Almanac Library, 2006.

Anderson, Dale. *World Almanac Library of the Civil War*. World Almanac Library, 2004.

Ashby, Ruth. *Presidents and First Ladies*. World Almanac Library, 2005.

Berg, Elizabeth. *United States* (Countries of the World). Gareth Stevens, 1999.

Brewer, Paul. *September 11 and Radical Islamic Terrorism* (Terrorism in Today's World). World Almanac Library, 2006.

Horn, Geoffrey M. *World Almanac Library of American Government*. World Almanac Library, 2003–2005.

Johnson, Michael. *Native Tribes of North America*. World Almanac Library, 2004.

Paul, Michael G. *Oklahoma City and Anti-Government Terrorism* (Terrorism in Today's World). World Almanac Library, 2006.

Stanley, George. *A Primary Source History of the United States*. World Almanac Library, 2005.

Steele, Christy. *America's Westward Expansion*. World Almanac Library, 2005.

Various authors. *America's Armed Forces*. World Almanac Library, 2005.

Various authors. *The American Experience in Vietnam*. World Almanac Library, 2005.

Various authors. *Landmark Events in American History*. World Almanac Library, 2003–2005.

Various authors. *World Almanac Library of the States*. World Almanac Library, 2003.

USEFUL WEB SITES

Official Site of the Navajo Nation
www.navajo.org/

United States Department of State: USINFO Publications
usinfo.state.gov/products/pubs/

U.S. Census Bureau
www.census.gov

United States Department of the Interior
www.doi.gov/kids/index.html

World Almanac for Kids: Presidents of the United States
www.worldalmanacforkids.com/explore/presidents.html

World Almanac for Kids: States
www.worldalmanacforkids.com/explore/states.html

World Almanac for Kids: U.S. History Timeline
www.worldalmanacforkids.com/explore/timeline.html

Index

Page numbers in **bold** indicate pictures.

About the Author

Sally Garrington is an experienced teacher of geography and a senior examiner for a major exam board. She has written books on the United States and Canada and regularly organizes geographical study tours for visitors to the United States.